P9-CQV-648

# CAREERS THAT COUNT

# EMERGENCY MEDICAL TECHNICIAN

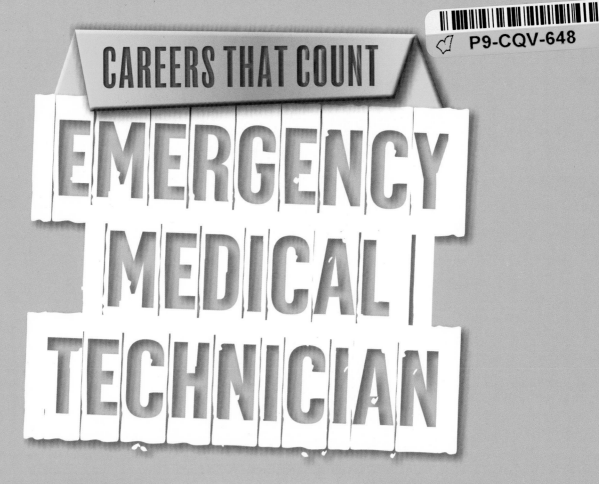

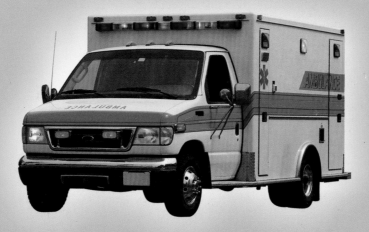

Louise Spilsbury

**PowerKiDS** press™

New York

Published in 2016 by **The Rosen Publishing Group**
29 East 21st Street, New York, NY 10010

Copyright © 2016 by The Rosen Publishing Group

All rights reserved. No part of this book may be reproduced in any form without permission in writing from the publisher, except by a reviewer.

Produced for Rosen by Calcium

Editors for Calcium: Sarah Eason and Jennifer Sanderson
Designer: Emma DeBanks

Picture credits: Cover: Shutterstock: Corepics VOF (top), Michael Jung (bottom); Inside: Dreamstime: Aprescindere 25t, Candybox Images 14, Tyler Olson 10, 20–21, Wellphotos 25b, Michael Zhang 19, Shutterstock: Air Images 20, Bikeriderlondon 13, Cleanfotos 11, Craig Stocks Arts 15, 18, Michael Jung 5, 22–23, 27, Lars Lindblad 2, 8, 26, Travis Manley 1, 6, 28, Maxstockphoto 24, Tyler Olson 7, 9, 16–17, Sjgh 4br.

Cataloging-in-Publication Data
Spilsbury, Louise.
Emergency medical technician / by Louise Spilsbury.
p. cm. — (Careers that count)
Includes index.
ISBN 978-1-4994-0809-6 (pbk.)
ISBN 978-1-4994-0808-9 (6 pack)
ISBN 978-1-4994-0807-2 (library binding)
1. Emergency medical technicians — Juvenile literature.
2. Emergency medicine — Juvenile literature. I. Spilsbury, Louise. II. Title.
RC86.5 S65 2016
616.02'5—d23

Manufactured in the United States of America
CPSIA Compliance Information: Batch WS15PK: For Further Information contact Rosen Publishing, New York, New York at 1-800-237-9932

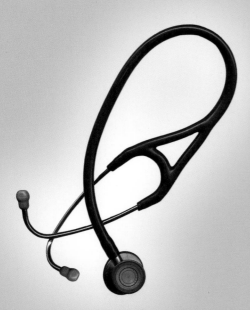

# CONTENTS

# WHICH CAREERS COUNT?

When people are choosing a career, what do you think matters most to them? Do you think how well a job pays is important to many people? Some people want a job that is interesting and pays well, but more than anything, they want to do something that makes a positive difference in the world. Careers that really count are those that make a difference in other people's lives. These are jobs in the **public service**, and include police officers, humanitarian aid workers, and firefighters.

## Serving the Public

Public-service careers not only make a difference to other people's lives, but the people who do them also get a lot of satisfaction from their work. The jobs can be challenging, difficult, and sometimes even dangerous. However, the people who do them are happy in their chosen career because they get satisfaction from helping others and being able to be use their knowledge, skills, and expertise. Some people work to save lives, investigate crimes, or rescue people from danger. In this book we will look at the work of emergency medical technicians (EMTs), heroes and heroines who save lives.

When there is a medical emergency, EMTs are ready to help.

## Careers That Count: A Career for You?

Here are three things you can do to figure out if a career that counts might be right for you.

- Know what you are good at doing. Think about what you like doing and what other people say you are good at.
- Know what type of work setting you like. Do you like being outdoors or at a desk? Do you like to work with people or do you prefer working alone?
- Find out about your chosen job and what it is really like. Reading this book is a good place to start.

# HEROES ON THE MOVE

EMTs do an incredibly important job. They help people who are injured or sick in many different situations. They give people immediate medical care before they can be taken to the hospital. EMTs are often the first to arrive at the scene of accidents, medical emergencies, and **natural disasters**. They give medical treatment to the victims of car crashes, to people hurt in an earthquake, and people who have suffered a medical emergency at home. EMTs perform life-saving treatments on patients to make sure they are **stable** before they are taken to the hospital.

## WHAT MAKES A GREAT EMT?

EMTs follow an **intensive** training program. They also carry out work experience to be certain they have all the skills they need for the job. However, there are also some important **characteristics** all EMTs need. They must be:

- Quick thinking: EMTs need to be able to quickly make decisions in difficult situations.
- Calm: EMTs need to keep calm when everyone around them may be panicking.
- Caring: EMTs must have a strong desire to help people.

Which of the above do you think is most important and why?

To save lives, EMTs have to stay calm and act quickly.

## Careers That Count: Becoming an EMT

There are some basic requirements that all EMTs must have before starting their career. They must be at least 18 years old and have a high school diploma or its equivalent. They will need to be **certified** by the National Registry of Emergency Medical Technicians (NREMT). To do this, EMTs must pass a written and practical exam. In some cases, EMTs may have to do math or reading test assessments and pass a medical examination, too.

# A TYPICAL DAY

There is no such thing as a typical day for EMTs! The number and types of calls vary from day to day. EMTs also work for different employers, from hospitals or medical centers to fire departments and private ambulance services. Here we look at the kind of day hospital EMTs might have during their 24-hour shift.

## AN EMT'S DAY

- **12 a.m.** At the start of a shift, EMTs check their ambulance. They complete a checklist to be sure that all their equipment is working, enough supplies are on hand, and the vehicle is ready.
- **2 a.m.** EMTs get some sleep.
- **4:45 a.m.** There is a call to an elderly man who has collapsed at his home. EMTs examine him and then take him to the hospital.
- **6 a.m.** Breakfast is eaten.
- **7 a.m.** EMTs complete chores at the station, like mopping the floors and cleaning their rest area.
- **9 a.m.** A call to a nursing home is answered. The patient is sick and must be transferred to the hospital.
- **11 a.m.** Another call is received, this time to a car accident. The victim is treated and taken to the hospital.
- **4 p.m.** EMTs rest or watch television. They also spend time on the computer, taking courses to keep their skills up-to-date.
- **10 p.m.** A call comes in. It is to a nightclub where there has been a fight. EMTs respond immediately.
- **12 a.m.** The shift ends.

## Careers That Count: Every Day Is Different

Every day working as an EMT is different. Some shifts may have no calls, while others may have so many that the EMT does not return to the ambulance station. Emergency services function 24 hours a day, so an EMT has irregular working hours.

Every day is different for EMTs so they must be prepared for all kinds of emergencies.

# RESPONDING TO CALLS

In an emergency, people dial 911 and speak to an operator. The operator then **dispatches** EMTs (and sometimes other emergency services) to the scene. EMTs answer calls to assist people in need every day. Emergency calls are urgent. People may be hurt or dying, and in need of urgent help. Responding to calls quickly and **efficiently** is vital for EMTs.

EMTs always wear their uniforms while they are on duty, so that when called to an emergency, they can race straight to their ambulance. They must drive very quickly to an emergency, so they turn on the ambulance's sirens and lights to warn drivers and pedestrians that they need to move out of the way. Ambulance drivers can go through red lights if necessary, as long as they do not put anyone in danger.

EMTs must drive quickly, but safely, to the scene of an emergency.

## Careers That Count: Knowing the Area

EMTs must take time to get to know the names of all the streets and major landmarks or buildings in their local area. This helps them respond to emergency calls quickly and efficiently.

# WHAT MAKES A GREAT EMT?

EMTs need to have a strong **work ethic**, which is a belief in the value and importance of hard work. They often have to respond to a lot of emergencies in a single day, at all hours, and even during vacations. How do you think having a strong work ethic helps EMTs handle the long hours, stress, and other demands that come with the job?

EMT ambulances have flashing lights and sirens to keep the public safe and help the EMTs get to an emergency swiftly.

# IN THE AMBULANCE

EMTs do not always spend a lot of time at the station. Sometimes, they mainly work from their ambulance so that they can remain **mobile** and travel to people who are in need. EMTs carry all the equipment they need to give people immediate medical assistance in the ambulance.

EMTs must learn how to use and maintain the emergency equipment found in their ambulances. These include:

- Heart **monitors** and **defibrillators** that are used to check patients with heart problems.
- Medical kits that carry supplies used to treat patients.
- **Stretchers** and boards that are used to move patients.
- Oxygen tanks that are used to treat patients who have breathing problems.
- **Splints** that are used to treat broken arms and legs.
- **Spinal collars** that hold the head and neck still. These are used if EMTs are concerned that the patient may have back or neck injuries.
- A **blood pressure** cuff that allows EMTs to measure and record a person's blood pressure.

## WHAT MAKES A GREAT EMT?

EMTs respond quickly to a call. They must drive the ambulance speedily to an emergency, and choose the equipment needed to treat patients. EMTs must keep cool, calm, and collected at all times. How do you think keeping calm when traveling to an **incident** and assisting people can help EMTs to do things quickly and safely?

EMTs must have the training and experience needed to understand how, and when, to use the different pieces of medical equipment in their ambulance.

Knowing which piece of equipment to use in the EMT ambulance is a matter of life and death.

# EXAMINING PATIENTS

As soon as they arrive at the scene of an accident or another medical emergency, EMTs must examine a patient carefully to figure out what immediate help is needed. It is important to make the patient stable so that he or she can be transported to a medical facility, where medical attention can be given.

EMTs must check if the patient is having trouble breathing. They must note if the patient is bleeding. If the patient is awake, the EMT can ask him or her questions about what happened, and about any medication being taken or medical history the EMT may need to know about. If the patient is not conscious, EMTs question those who are present at the scene. Along with the physical examination, this helps the EMT decide what is wrong and what action to take next.

Examining a patient carefully is important. It helps EMTs make the right choice of treatment.

## Careers That Count: Training Procedures

EMTs are trained in what **procedures** to follow when examining a patient, so they know what to check first. They are trained to follow medical **protocols** and guidelines. This helps them check for vital information that is needed to keep a patient safe.

# WHAT MAKES A GREAT EMT?

EMTs need to be **empathetic**. They need to be caring and understanding. How do you think being empathetic can help when dealing with people who are hurt and upset?

Treating people with kindness and consideration is part of an EMT's role.

# EVERYDAY EMERGENCIES

Most calls that EMTs attend to may not be as dramatic as those shown on television, but they still are very important. EMTs must be prepared for anything because they may have to assist in many kinds of emergencies. They may help a woman give birth or help someone who has breathing problems. They may treat someone who is a **diabetic** or who has had an **allergic reaction** to a substance.

EMTs also provide transportation for patients from one medical center or hospital to another. These transfers are common if the EMTs work for private ambulance services. Patients often need to be taken to a hospital that specializes in their injuries or illness. They may need to be transported to a nursing home. This usually happens when a patient is unable to move easily. EMTs must often enter people's homes and lift them onto stretchers so they can be taken to the hospital.

## WHAT MAKES A GREAT EMT?

EMTs must have good **time-management skills**. EMTs have work to do at the station, scheduled trips to transport patients, and they must respond quickly to all emergencies. How do you think having strong time-management skills can help EMTs do so many jobs quickly and efficiently?

It is important to transport fragile, elderly, or sick patients between medical centers with care.

## Careers That Count: Lifting and Moving

EMTs are trained to lift and carry patients in a way that does not risk hurting either the patient or themselves. To lift and move people correctly, at least two EMTs must work together. The patient must be carefully strapped to a stretcher, and the correct lifting techniques must be used to move him or her.

# SAVING LIVES

EMTs are usually the first people at an emergency scene, and they often take steps that save lives. When called out to an incident, they make decisions and give treatments that keep people alive. They often do so while dealing not only with the patient, but often also with distressed family members or bystanders.

In an emergency, EMTs often work together to save a patient's life.

## Careers That Count: Gaining Experience

Unlike hospital staff, EMTs must provide life-saving medical care with only the equipment they have in the ambulance. They usually have the help of just one other EMT, and must work in a great variety of situations. That is why, along with studying techniques in the classroom, inexperienced EMTs also train by working alongside experienced EMTs. This helps them learn how to think and act quickly in response to each unique case.

## WHAT MAKES A GREAT EMT?

EMTs often face upsetting situations, such as horrific injuries at a crash scene or a natural disaster. How do you think EMTs prepare themselves to cope with some of the distressing things they see when they are on duty?

After examining a patient and finding that he or she is in a life-threatening situation, EMTs must decide what action to take. Sometimes this means controlling heavy bleeding, treating **shock**, and bandaging wounds. If the patient is not breathing, this may mean tilting the head and clearing the airways of any blockage. The patient's **pulse** is taken to see if the heart is still pumping blood through the **veins**. If there is no pulse, EMTs must restart the heart beating, for example, by performing **CPR**.

This EMT is putting an oxygen mask on a patient to help her breathe.

# CRASH SCENES

When EMTs respond to an automobile accident on the freeway, the scene is likely to be noisy and busy. With traffic quickly passing by, it may also be dangerous. EMTs have to keep a cool head and assess the situation quickly. In a car crash in which several people may be injured, the EMTs must decide who is in the most urgent need of help, and treat them before responding to others.

## WHAT MAKES A GREAT EMT?

EMTs have to **communicate** with patients, other EMTs, the public, and other emergency service workers under stressful situations. How do you think being able to pass on messages quickly and clearly, while also being a good listener and observer, can help EMTs gather vital information?

EMTs often have to work with other emergency services at a crash scene. For example, if a victim is trapped in a car, the fire department cuts open the car. While waiting for the firefighters, EMTs examine and treat the victim as best they can. They check **vital signs**, and often put on a spinal collar until a back injury is ruled out. Once the victim is removed from the car, the EMTs put him or her on to a **backboard**. The victim is then moved into the ambulance.

EMTs work quickly at a crash scene and often have to rush injured people to the nearest hospital for treatment.

## Careers That Count: Physical Training

EMTs may be required to pull an injured person out of a crushed car or fallen structure. The work is physically demanding because heavy lifting, kneeling, and getting up and down are requirements for the job. EMTs must keep themselves fit and strong in order to carry out their jobs.

# AT THE HOSPITAL

When EMTs have made sure a patient is stable after an emergency or made someone comfortable after a fall, they drive the patient to the hospital. For example, when a child has broken an arm, the EMTs put a splint around the broken bone, check for shock or other injuries, and then take the child to a hospital where the broken bone can be x-rayed and set.

On the way to the hospital, EMTs make sure that the patient has no other health problems, and that he or she is as comfortable as possible. They watch the patient's blood pressure, heart rate, and breathing patterns. At the hospital or medical center, EMTs wait with the patient until he or she can be taken to the emergency department. EMTs tell emergency department staff about the incident, the patient, and what actions were taken. When they leave, EMTs clean the stretcher, replace used supplies, and check equipment so they are ready for the next call.

EMTs keep working on patients all the way to the hospital, to keep the patients comfortable and safe.

## Careers That Count: Paperwork

After every call, EMTs have to fill out paperwork. They have to record when and where the incident happened, who was involved, the medical condition and history of the patient, and what actions were taken. They also have to make note of what supplies they used and other information, including the patient's billing and insurance information.

## WHAT MAKES A GREAT EMT?

EMTs need to be emotionally stable. That means they need to be caring, but not get too upset by other people's distress. How do you think controlling their emotions helps EMTs deal with life-or-death situations and suffering patients?

# TRAINING DAYS

To do their job well, EMTs must have a high level of education and experience. However, new medical treatments and technologies are being discovered and designed all the time. It is therefore vital that EMTs keep training throughout their career, to make sure they can do their very best for the patients in their care.

EMTs must maintain their certification every two to three years, through continuing emergency medical training. This may include written and practical tests, to check their knowledge and skills as well as their abilities in emergency situations. EMTs may also choose to do advanced education programs. These allow them to become **supervisors**, instructors, or physician assistants if and when they want to move on from their EMT roles.

EMTs learn to do some treatments, like CPR, on dummies. This EMT is learning how to check that a patient's airways are clear.

## WHAT MAKES A GREAT EMT?

EMTs must be motivated. They must really want to do their job well because they have to work hard and must also keep training to keep their skills up-to-date. How do you think being motivated helps when studying and attending courses to learn new skills?

Before connecting medical equipment to people, EMTs first practice fitting them onto dummies.

## Careers That Count: Becoming a Paramedic

EMTs provide basic life support in a prehospital setting to patients during medical emergencies. **Paramedics** receive more advanced training, and they can carry out more treatments than EMTs are qualified to do. Some EMTs complete additional training and certification courses to become paramedics.

# RISKS AND REWARDS

Working as an EMT can be tough, both physically and mentally. Most of the time an EMT is not in any personal danger, apart from the risks of being hurt when lifting a patient. However, there are times when an EMT does face dangerous situations. These include dealing with victims of a traffic accident on a busy road or being called to help someone with gunshot wounds in a dangerous or unsafe area.

As long as an EMT follows established safety measures, the risks of being injured are greatly reduced and it is rare that an EMT comes to any harm. The rewards of being an EMT, on the other hand, are great. Most of the time, an EMT will find his or her work exciting and challenging and, above all, will enjoy the opportunity to help others.

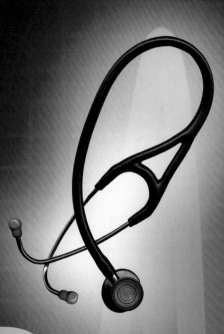

## Careers That Count: Keeping Safe

EMTs learn about the science of infections, such as the different types of infections and how they are passed on. This knowledge, and learning how to properly clean and **disinfect** equipment, helps EMTs to keep themselves safe from catching infections while dealing with diseased patients.

At the end of each working day, EMTs know that they have done an important job. They know that theirs is a career that counts.

## WHAT MAKES A GREAT EMT?

EMTs are not particularly well-paid, and they do not always get the thanks they deserve for the amazing job they do. However, they are **dedicated** and determined people who have a strong desire to help others and do their job to the best of their ability. Could you have the dedication and determination it takes to be a great EMT?

# COULD YOU HAVE A CAREER THAT COUNTS?

Do you want to become an EMT? These are the steps you would need to take to reach your goal.

**Subjects to study at school:** You do not need to study particular subjects, but math and science will be useful. Take opportunities to practice teamwork while at school, and to mix and deal with people from a wide range of backgrounds.

**Work experience:** Volunteering at a local hospital can help you find out what it is like to work in the medical field. It can also help you to practice working and communicating with patients. This kind of volunteer experience may also help an EMT stand out when applying for a job.

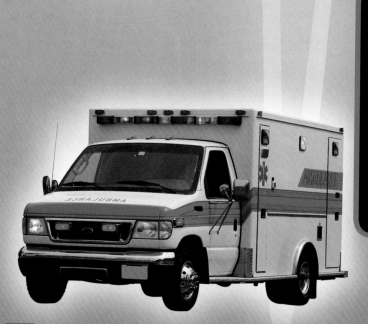

**Exams to pass:** To become an EMT you must have a high school diploma or an equivalent degree.

**College:** Training programs are available at EMT academies, community colleges, technical schools, and universities. These programs help prepare aspiring EMTs for the appropriate NREMT certification exam.

**Improve your résumé:** Volunteer in your community. Do not volunteer just to increase your chances of getting a job, but because you have a real interest in caring for your fellow citizens. This will also show that you want to care for people in your community.

**Life experience:** Get fit and stay fit. EMTs need to be physically fit and strong. It will also help to get your driver's license, too.

**Getting the job:** All EMTs must be at least 18 years old and hold a current CPR certification. There are two types of EMT qualification: basic and intermediate. Training programs may include up to 350 hours of classroom and practical learning. After the training is complete, you will be ready to apply for a job as a qualified EMT.

# GLOSSARY

**allergic reaction** When someone reacts badly to a usually harmless substance. The person may develop a rash or even stop breathing.

**backboard** A board used to support or straighten a person's back, especially after an accident.

**blood pressure** The strength of a person's blood pushing against the sides of his or her veins.

**certified** To have a certificate saying that a person is fully qualified to do something.

**characteristics** Features or qualities belonging to a particular person or thing.

**communicate** To give and receive information.

**CPR** An acronym for cardiopulmonary resuscitation. CPR is a first aid technique that can be used if someone is not breathing properly or if his or her heart has stopped.

**dedicated** Devoted and completely committed to something.

**defibrillators** Devices that start the heart beating properly again.

**diabetic** Someone suffering from diabetes, which is a condition that causes a person's blood sugar level to become too high.

**disinfect** To destroy germs that can cause disease and infections.

**dispatches** Sends out.

**efficiently** Well and quickly.

**empathetic** Having the ability to share another person's feelings.

**employers** People who pay others to do work.

**incident** An accident or dangerous event.

**intensive** Involving a lot of effort or work.

**mobile** Able to move around easily.

**monitors** Machines for checking something, such as a person's heart rate.

**natural disasters** Events such as floods, earthquakes, and hurricanes that cause great damage or loss of life.

**paramedics** People who have medical training to deal with injured people at accident sites.

**procedures** Series of actions done in a certain order.

**protocols** Official ways of doing things.

**public service** Something that is done to help people rather than to make a profit.

**pulse** Throbbing that can be felt as blood passes through a major vein, for example, in the wrist.

**shift** A time period in which different groups of workers take turns doing the same jobs.

**shock** A life-threatening condition that occurs when blood loss stops vital organs, like the brain and heart, working properly.

**spinal collars** Devices used to support a patient's neck and head.

**splints** Strips of hard material used to support broken bones.

**stable** Not changing.

**stretchers** Devices used for carrying patients lying down.

**supervisors** People in charge of other workers.

**time-management skills** The ability to plan and control the amount of time a person spends on different tasks to make the most of his or her working day.

**veins** The tubes that carry blood around the inside of the body.

**vital signs** Important body functions such as breathing and heartbeat.

**work ethic** A belief in the value and importance of work.

**x-rayed** Made an image of the inside of the body using an x-ray.

# FURTHER READING

Greve, Tom. *EMT: Crisis Care for Injuries and Illness* (Emergency Response). Vero Beach, FL: Rourke Publishing Group, 2014.

Murray, Aaron R. *EMTs Help Us* (All About Community Helpers). Berkeley Heights, NJ: Enslow Elementary, 2012.

Ollhoff, Jim. *EMT* (Emergency Workers). Edina, MN: ABDO & Daughters, 2012.

Shepherd, Jodie. *A Day With Paramedics* (Rookie Read-About Community). New York, NY: Scholastic, 2012.

# WEBSITES

Due to the changing nature of Internet links, PowerKids Press has developed an online list of websites related to the subject of this book. This site is updated regularly. Please use this link to access the list: **www.powerkidslinks.com/ctc/emt**

# INDEX